MORE THAN JUST A GAME: OVERCOMING ADVERSITY

Written by: Kyvin Goodin-Rogers

Edited by: Dana G. Fisher

Table of Contents

PREFACE

In my book, I discuss both my experiences and how they have changed me over time. This gives you a glimpse of what I had to overcome over the years to get to where I am today. I am very thankful for everyone that I have encountered in my life as I was able to learn from every one of them. I am blessed to be able to share my story with you. The purpose of this book is to show you that you are not what happened to you, therefore, never give up on your dreams. I know that many athletes have been through something like what I've been through and I want them to know that you're going to go through some tough times but you can't let those times keep you down or let them make you feel any less than you are. Whatever is said about you or done to you, it won't define you. Life lessons are blessings in disguise. Do what you are called to do, and don't let anybody get in your way. Whatever is meant for you will always be for you.

Kyvin Goodin-Rogers

CHAPTER 1

I have thought of a million different ways to tell this story. It hasn't been the easiest story to tell. But I've finally built up the courage to tell the story the only way I know how to tell it - and that's from the heart.

Growing up I fell in love with basketball so much that it became a part of my identity. On the court is where I felt at peace. When my teammates and I stepped between those four lines, nothing else mattered. Everyone played with a purpose, we fought for a purpose and we always had each other's back. It was a great feeling leaving imprints on people's lives by showing them what it felt like to love through the game of basketball. Despite what the outsiders had to say, we made statements and accomplished many goals. When we came together, we became one. We were surrounded by a coaching staff whose mission was to get better every day, win championships, and to grow our character. They were very supportive and had their best interest in each person on the team. I knew what it took to be on a team and to become a great teammate. I understood what was needed to bring everyone together to accomplish goals. If you don't believe me, check my resume:

At Lebanon Middle School, we won the 7th grade State Tournament where we went 27-0, and in 8th grade we won the Middle School State tournament again and went 33-0. In high school, we won six District titles, one Region runner-up along with four Region championships. In the KHSAA State Tournament, we were in the Sweet Sixteen, Elite Eight, and Final Four.

But what I didn't know was that this new path that I was about to take into college would have many obstacles that would make into who I am today. I didn't know that my character, my heart, mind, body, and soul would be tested on a whole other level. On this new adventure, my expectation was this is a time to get a degree, learn more, meet new people, train for championships and prepare for the

WNBA. This was a time to break generational curses and to be able to provide for my family.

But instead I found something else...

CHAPTER 2

During my junior year in high school, I scheduled an unofficial visit with the University of Kentucky. Honestly, I couldn't believe that I was going on a visit there, considering I'd grown up a Louisville Cardinals fan ever since my dad, Tick Rogers, played basketball at the University of Louisville from 1992-1996. I had spoken to some of the University of Kentucky coaches and it made me want to explore my options with the university, so I took an unofficial visit. For those of you who may be unfamiliar with what an unofficial visit is, it is when a student athlete can visit a coach on the coach's campus at any time, as long as the student athlete pays their own way.

Overall it was a good visit. I met the staff, went out to eat with the coaches and toured the campus. The unofficial visit was great and it was time for it to come to an end. As my mom, step-dad and I sat in the office with the coaches, we talked about how the University of Kentucky could be a great fit for me considering I liked it there, I liked how they seemed to care for one another and welcomed others like family. Not to mention they played my style of basketball, what more could I ask for? This seemed like the perfect fit, and I wanted to be a part of it so I committed right there on the spot. I hadn't spoken to anyone about this decision before the visit, however I was very confident I had made the right decision.

Word had gotten around that I verbally committed to play basketball at the University of Kentucky. But I couldn't let that distract me. I still had other things to accomplish before I could ever think about stepping foot on campus.

The one thing I hadn't accomplished yet that I wanted to do before I went to college was to win a state championship. We had already won several district and region titles. We even made it to state the past three years in a row. Every year we were one step closer to our goal. Senior year was the year that determined if we could win the state championship.

I had coaches that knew how to prepare me. No, I was not perfect, but what I can say is that I always came to the gym and gave my best. It didn't matter how I felt, I would give the best I could that day. I took every day, day by day. All I knew how to do was work and trust the process. My team was viewed as the Division I high school team; it wasn't a team you got to see every day in high school. We were a team that worked hard all the time, and we had coaches who loved the game. They knew how to make us work hard and go for what we wanted, and it showed on the court.

My senior season our hard work paid off. Not only did we finally win the KHSAA State Tournament, but we went 39-0 and ranked #4 in the Nation! We made history! After working hard all season, we got what we had been working for. Just to give some context, when I started playing basketball with Marion County the summer going into my 7th grade year, I couldn't even do a left-handed layup, let alone walk and chew gum at the same time. A record of 39-0 was crazy! I remember thinking if this was possible then there's no telling what's going to happen when I get to play at the next level. Hard work really does pay off despite everything that you must go through to get to where you want to be.

CHAPTER 3

Have you ever wished for a moment to come, and when it comes you become nervous and scared? That was me when it was time to move on campus. It was the summer of June 2013 when myself, along with my best friend since 7th grade, Makayla Epps (who had also committed to playing basketball at UK) moved onto campus early for summer workouts and classes. We started school before the average freshman did, considering we had graduated on May 24th and would start college in two weeks. During those two weeks we also had to attend Kentucky All-Stars for one week.

College life was very challenging at first. Having to do 6am strength and conditioning, classes, manage meals, and attending tutors was not easy. It was not a schedule I was used to. There were workouts that I thought would kill me at times. That was the hardest part about being a freshman; the adjustment. But when you really want something you will do what you need to do. It gives you structure and accountability. I began to learn and I adjusted. The three words that I heard every day were Honesty, Hard Work, and Discipline. I saw these words hung on walls in the locker room, on our shirts, coach's office, and in the practice gym. Coach reminded us every day it was our motto that we stood by. Those were the three words that I lived by and still do until this day.

School then became a little easier. I could manage my tutors, classes, and homework better, along with basketball. The workouts and practices were getting better. I was eating healthier and becoming stronger, and it felt good. I started to really enjoy it once I could see changes. All the work that comes with these things aren't always fun, but they are worth it in the end.

After working all summer to improve my skills, strength, and condition, it was now time for season to begin. Do you know how long I've waited for this moment? It was finally about to begin.

Little did I know, three days before our first game I would have a life-changing experience. For the past couple of weeks, I had been having severe chest pain. Each time I would inhale I would feel a sharp pain shooting through my chest. I told the trainer about what I was experiencing, and at first they thought I was out of shape but I knew that wasn't the case. I kept doing my workouts and practicing hoping that it would pass over. The trainer took me to a cardiologist to get my heart checked and everything came back normal. They kept treating it as asthma, but something deep down told me it was not my asthma either but we kept treating it as asthma.

One early morning at about 4:30 am the chest pain woke me up out of my sleep. It felt like someone was sticking a nail into my chest every time that I would breathe in. The pain was so intense that I cried and rolled over to grab my inhaler. After I used the inhaler, I rolled back over and tried going back to sleep; considering I had to be up in two hours for weight lifting and practice.

Time passed and my alarm went off. I woke, got ready, grabbed some breakfast and walked over to the practice gym for weights and team practice. I walked over with my teammate and told her the trouble I was having with my chest. She told me "Girl, go tell the trainer and get checked out." I told her "I've already told them before, but this is the worst that I've felt." Once I went into the gym, I got dressed for weights and headed inside the weight room. Before I knew it, my trainer was walking into the weight room too. Come to find out, my teammate told the trainer what was going on. She began asking me what was wrong and told me I looked pale. I told her the pain that I was feeling in my chest and how bad it hurt to breathe. She suggested that we go into the training room so that she could check me out. Once we got inside she had me lie down on my back, crossed my arms across my chest and asked, "Does that hurt?" My response was "No… it only hurts when I inhale."

She continued to do more stretches. Each time I breathed in I felt like I was dying. She then told me to go into the practice gym and watch practice until we could leave and go to the doctor. About thirty minutes later she walked into the gym to tell me that it was time to go. I ran into the locker room to change clothes to get ready for the doctor. Once I arrived, the doctor performed a blood test along with a series of other tests. After that was finished the nurse told me they would contact me later about the results.

When I returned to campus, I went about my regular schedule for the day which included classes, tutors, and an academic meeting with my academic coach. As I was leaving from my academic coach's office I got the call - a call that I didn't really understand at first. After we hung up I called my trainer and relayed to her about how they thought I had a blood clot and wanted me to come back to the hospital. I met with my trainer and headed to the hospital. I called my mom to let her know what was going on. She told me she was on her way.

At the time, I didn't realize how serious a blood clot was so I was still trying to figure out why my mom sounded so frightened on the phone. Everyone else around me seemed so calm, so I never once thought that I was at risk. But I remained calm and went to the hospital and waited to be called back.

CHAPTER 4

After I was admitted to University of

Kentucky Hospital I was lying in bed trying to wrap

my head around what was happening. I just

couldn't understand, but I knew how strong I was

and I wasn't going down without a fight. I wasn't

going to let this get me down and hold me back.

Within a few minutes, my mom and step-dad came

walking in. We chatted for a while and in walked

the nurse. She told me I needed to get three shots

in my stomach. It was the absolute worst feeling

ever. To make matters worse, I also found out I

would be getting a shot in my stomach every twelve

hours for the rest of the week. I hated the thought

of this but I decided not to worry about it, and focus on what was in front of me. Then Coach walked into the room. We talked for a bit, and at the end of the conversation I remember looking at him smiling and said, "It's okay Coach, I'll be back at practice tomorrow."

The next words that I heard literally ripped my heart right out of my chest. The nurse said, "I'm sorry, but I don't think you will be allowed to play this season." DO WHAT? I literally almost cried. No one has ever told me I couldn't play for an entire season. This must be a joke. This can't be real life. What did I do to deserve this? I felt empty. I felt like I was living a bad dream. The doctors discovered I had a pulmonary embolism, which is a blood clot in the lung. If left untreated it can travel to the heart and lead to death. Why me?

After everyone left the room I was thinking about what could have been. I felt like I was failing already. I'm not sure why I felt this way. Maybe it was because basketball was a huge part of my life, and it felt like it was being taken away. I started feeling like an outsider, why do I feel this way? It could have been because I felt like I couldn't play a role on the team anymore, which was not true but at the time that's how I felt.

There were so many emotions going around in my head at the moment. But everything changed when my teammates came walking in. I almost cried again. I was so happy to see them. My teammates showed they cared about me, and I couldn't have been happier.

A few days passed and I was finally released from the hospital. I was up and moving and ready to get back on the court. That's all I could think about. I tried to remain positive during this time, and although it wasn't easy, I made it. It was a hard situation to deal with because you feel like an outsider when you cannot participate at 100%. During practice, I was not allowed to make physical contact on the court due to being on blood thinners but I still worked on my individual game. I took this time to learn the game and learned how I could help. For the first time, I could break down the game and really understand it. I was like a sponge taking in every little detail as much as possible. I realized that I may not have been able to do anything physically, but mentally there was a lot that I could do. Sitting out my entire freshman season due to the blood clot was an eye-opener for me - it made me realize that you can't take anything for granted because in the blink of an eye it can be gone.

After many months of hard work and persistence, I was finally released to play again. It was one of the best feelings ever. My time had finally come, Thank

God! I had to prove that I really wanted this, so that's what I did. Before I knew it, my sophomore season was starting and I was in the starting lineup. I felt like my hard work had paid off.

For me this was a big accomplishment. Growing up all I heard was *Don't expect a lot of playing time your freshman year, that's hard to do.* Not only did I not touch the floor my freshman year due to my blood clot, but I'm a starter on the team. What are the odds of this? I was grateful, not only for surviving through the blood clot, but also finally getting the chance to play with my team.

CHAPTER 5

During the 2014-2015 season, my sophomore year, I started 15 of my 34 games. Everything was going very well. I regained my confidence with a crazy work ethic. I was determined to return to the team with a vengeance. I averaged 4.2 points and 3.1 rebounds per game, and ranked third most on the team from the 3–point line, shooting at 35.4 percent - averaging at least one 3-pointer per game.

What no one knew was that I was facing some obstacles, once again. Before my starting streak ended I was having problems with my right knee. I had already told the trainer about it and she recommended I do some rehab and not do extra individual workouts. So that's what I did.

One night I got a phone call from my position coach. He called to tell me to come to the individual workout. I told him I wasn't coming because my knee was still hurting from the practice earlier that day, and the trainer told me not to do extra workouts until my knee was feeling better. I was going to skip that night's workout so I could soak it in ice and get it somewhat ready for the next day. Apparently what I told him wasn't good enough and he began accusing me of not wanting to improve my skills. He then told me that I was basically stealing money from the school, and that since I didn't want to work and get better that I was going to lose my starting spot. This hurt me a lot considering I was in love with this game. It didn't make sense to me on how he could say something like that to me when I came to every workout even when I wasn't feeling it. This game was my life. I had sacrificed a lot for this game. How could he say such a thing? It messed with me mentally.

I had never felt this way before. All I wanted to do was make my knee feel better. Why was this such a big deal? Why is he talking to me this way? Was it wrong for me to say no to take care of my knee? Why isn't anyone listening to me? Are they really going to bench me?

The next day before practice, the team and coaches walked into the film room for film, and just before I was getting ready to walk onto the court for practice, Coach stopped me. We began to talk and during our conversation he said I would be losing my starting spot because I needed more work and he felt like it would the right thing to do. In my head, I could not believe what was happening.

But instead of getting mad I just smiled and said, "I got you Coach" and headed on to practice. Even though I may not have shown it on the outside, I was beyond devastated. I felt like I was in the back after all the work I did. Whenever he told me to jump I asked how high. I've been preached to my whole life about respecting others, but what about me? I'm trying to be the best person possible and this is how I'm done?

I just wanted to make the coaches happy and give them all I had and I felt like I never got anything in return. Do I sit here and take this or step up and say something? But from my past meetings with Coach, I honestly didn't feel safe. I knew he wouldn't listen so I backed down and just took it. I couldn't understand why I was suffering from knee pain that I'd mentioned to them, but still hadn't got the help that I needed.

Behind closed doors I felt belittled, unworthy and not enough. I felt like no one really cared about me unless I could give them what they wanted.

CHAPTER 6

The season had passed and I'm to the point where I feel like I'm dragging my leg behind me. I had been fighting to get my knee checked out and it hadn't happened yet, so I decided to schedule my own appointment to see what was wrong with it. By this time, I'm just searching for answers and for someone to listen. I was so frustrated.

After completing a series of tests, the doctor gave me the results. I felt better, well, a little better. By this point, I had grown tired of explaining my knee issue and it being dismissed with telling me everything would be okay. It felt like my plea to be heard was being ignored. Even during the time I had my chest pain, no one was listening until it was almost too late, and now this. I knew I wasn't crazy or over-reacting. But, why wasn't anyone listening?

I took the results to my trainer and explained what the doctor said. She looked over them and said there was nothing they could do until we had gotten a second opinion from a doctor at the university. I told her that was fine and she got in touch with a physician so that we could get a second opinion. After I got my second opinion from that doctor, it came time to schedule an appointment for knee surgery. I was a complete nervous wreck but so happy at the same time. I was ready to become pain-free again. I knew after this surgery that everything would be okay again.

After my surgery, I had about six weeks of physical therapy. If anyone knows about physical therapy, you know how hard it can be sometimes trying to push through. For me, this was my first surgery and I didn't know what to expect afterwards. I just had to trust the people around me to get me where I needed to be. During my physical therapy time with my trainer I would ask questions just to learn more about my situation. But there was one question that I would ask almost every day *"Why do I feel the same exact pain I had before surgery?"* and the only answer I would get back was "You're going to have pain, it's part of the process." How am I supposed to feel the same exact pain I felt before surgery? What does that even mean? I was confused, to say the least... But nevertheless, I continued to trust them.

As time went on and I could rest my knee, my pain decreased, but as soon as it was time to work out again that same pain returned. In my mind, all I could think was, why in the world does my knee feel like it's never been fixed? I can't be crazy... there is no way possible this is how it's supposed to be.

CHAPTER 7

It was now the beginning of my junior season and I was still having trouble with my knee, but I hadn't let it stop me. I was still doing everything that was asked of me. Even though I still struggled to get up and down the court, I got it done. Right about now you may be asking why I was still practicing. I kept practicing because when I said something about my knee hurting and asked to sit out for a bit, I was made to feel guilty about it. They said it was mental. In their eyes, I wasn't going hard enough. No matter what I did, nothing was good enough. I thought, this is too much. I was at my breaking point.

A couple days later, we played Arizona State and during the game I suffered a concussion. My teammate and I went up for a rebound, and when she came down she elbowed me in the side of my head. I ended up having to sit out a couple games, which I thought was a good thing. At least this would give me some time to rest my knee and hopefully ease the pain. After a week or so I passed my concussion test and I was able to play in both the Colorado and Eastern Michigan games. At this point I didn't feel the same anymore. I started recognizing how unhappy I really was. I was beginning to hate the game that I loved so much. The game that helped me take a break from real life was not only bringing me physical pain, but mental pain as well. I wasn't happy and in serious knee

pain. As a matter of fact, I was tired of acting like I

was happy.

What I decided to do was stop trying to fix things

on my own and depending on others, and instead

try something different. Right before my last game

against Jackson State, I said a prayer.

"God, if I'm not supposed to be here

anymore please give me a sign."

At the time, I wasn't much on prayer, Honestly, I

didn't think it would work. Once the game ended

God had already answered my prayers. He revealed

to me that it was time to go. It was a feeling of *It's*

time to go, know that this is not the end. It won't

always feel good, but trust me. As we sang the fight

song at the end of the game like we always did, I

leaned over to Makayla and told her that I was

transferring. Her eyes got wide, jaw dropped and

she fixed her mouth to say "No". I felt so bad, I

didn't know what to do.

I went into the locker room and changed, walked

up to my mom in the bleachers and said, "It's time

to go."

She looked at me and said "OK, let's go" and

gathered her things to leave. She didn't know that

leaving from the game wasn't the only thing I

meant.

I told her "No, I'm ready to transfer."

That night I called Coach and explained that I wanted to have a meeting with him the next day. He asked why, but I wanted to wait and do it in person. I scheduled the meeting and my mom and dad agreed to come with me. We went to Coach's office and sat down with him to discuss my decision.

I told Coach I wasn't happy and that I wanted to transfer. He asked why, I told him that I was still having knee pain, I felt like my concerns weren't heard, and I felt like it's just time for me to go. He said, "I hate to see you go" and came over to give me a hug. Then he walked us to the door. He said I would be given a full release, wished me well and we went on our way.

My parents and I were almost back to our vehicles when I saw my teammates Makayla and Linnae walking up the sidewalk. Without saying a word, the look on their face, they already knew what had just happened. Looking at both of them, it was crazy that we would no longer be playing together on the same team. This really crushed me a lot because the three of us had become so close on and off the court. We had an unbreakable bond. And especially with Makayla, my best friend that I'd played basketball with since middle school, it was one of the hardest things for me. It took everything in me not to cry. After playing together for eight years, it was coming to an end. And boy did it hurt like hell. I felt like I let her down because I was supposed to be her backbone through the good and the bad and here I was transferring. I felt so bad.

It came to a point where we avoided seeing each other face-to-face because it hurt too much, and we knew we would cry. Not only were we teammates, we were sisters. We had always and will always have each other's back. We had been through so much already. One of the hardest parts about leaving was leaving her because I knew we had started this thing together and we wanted to finish it together. Not only was it hard to leave my best friend, but it was hard to leave all of my teammates. We had been through so much together and built bonds that could never be broken. When we would have our days where we didn't know what to do we would tell each other "Keeping pushing, we got this, fake it until you make it." We lifted one another up and challenged each other. I don't know what I would've done without them by my side. From day one they welcomed me with open arms and I'm thankful for that.

After my parents left and went back to work, I received a phone call from my coach asking me to come back to his office to talk to him about my decision. I was a little skeptical, even a bit nervous. But nonetheless, I agreed to meet up. I figured we could have a sit-down discussion with just the two of us so that I could explain why I had chosen to leave. If nothing else, this should clear the air.

I walked back into the office. As soon as I had sat down, the whole atmosphere changed. Suddenly things took a sharp turn. It wasn't the same conversation we had just half an hour ago. After I left from the office the second time, I felt empty. I was numb. It was the lowest I'd ever felt in my life. All I knew was that I didn't want to feel this way anymore. At this point, not only would I need to regain my confidence as a basketball player, but it was even more crucial that I do the same for my

mental well-being. That exit meeting was the

beginning of what caused a lot of mental turmoil

which lasted for a quite a while. But, in the

meantime, my next task was to find a school to

transfer to where I could get a new start.

This time my focus was, where can I go that I know

that will be taken seriously and can grow?

CHAPTER 8

One person popped in mind, someone I thought I could trust with the end of my college career. That special person was Michelle Clark-Heard. Before I committed to UK, I was introduced to her when I verbally committed to the University of Louisville where she was an assistant coach. She was a down-to-earth person with a loving spirit. I loved how she cared for the people she loved, and I knew that was what I needed at that time. Michelle Clark-Heard was now the head coach at Western Kentucky University where I would play my senior season.

My trust issues were all the way jacked up, but for some reason I trusted her so I basically ran to her and didn't even attempt to look at any other schools. She welcomed me with open arms. I was scared and hurt, and all I wanted was to play ball with someone who had their best intentions for players.

Once I moved onto campus at the end of December 2015, we had several meetings, but the one that I remember most was when we talked about winning championships. I remember telling her that's what I wanted, and I promised her that we would win one before I left. I decided this will be a chance to get better and learn since I had to sit out a year due to transfer rules. When a student athlete transfers from one school to another, they are not allowed to play for one year, nor travel with the team. The only options are to practice and attend classes. But after a couple of practices I started to question if I would be able to run. My pain hadn't gotten any better, and I was tired of feeling this way. Then I thought, maybe I shouldn't have promised her a Conference Championship. I was in so much pain I was starting to second-guess what I said, and the last thing I wanted to do was to let anyone down. I decided to tell Coach Clark-Heard that I was having knee issues and I wasn't sure how effective I would be.

She discussed the options I could take. We decided to get my knee checked out again before I continued to practice with my new team. I wasn't happy, not one bit. People say you should be grateful, and yes, I was very grateful but have you ever loved something so much and it felt like it was slipping away and you try everything in your power to keep it from slipping away that you lose yourself during the process of trying to fix it? It was a battle every day! People were only able to see the physical battle that I was facing, they couldn't see the battle that was going on in my head.

Little did I know, I was going to have to keep fighting because my battle wasn't over yet.

After talking with Coach Clark-Heard and my trainer we made an appointment to see the team doctor. Just to back-track a bit, while I was at UK I had gone to see my own doctor. The results he gave me showed everything that needed to be done during surgery. Fast forward a bit, once I had already settled in at Western and went to see their team doctor, I found out that the knee surgery I had wasn't completed correctly. As a matter of fact, they only did half of my surgery. *Half of my knee surgery? Really? Why?* To this day, I'm still not sure why, and I may never know why. All I know is it still haunts me. How can this be possible? Is this even allowed?

I couldn't believe it. This meant I would have to have another knee surgery to try and clean up the first one. It finally made sense. That was the reason I was having all that knee pain after surgery! I knew I wasn't crazy. I was so mad. I became bitter. I was literally faking it until I made it at this point. I didn't know what to do. My emotions were all over the place. After all this time, after everything I've done this is how it has to be? I was broken, it hurt like hell.

I eventually had to snap back and find a way to get through this next knee surgery. I was so frustrated. But as usual I did what I had to do to make it through. Luckily, I had just transferred so I had to sit out a year anyway, so I guess everything happens for a reason at the end of the day.

It was January of 2016 when I had my knee surgery. This was my second knee surgery in a year. It wasn't easy. I still couldn't wrap my head around this whole thing. It was overwhelming. After sitting out for several weeks and going through physical therapy and everything else that comes with surgery, I was finally able to get back to practice. I was happy, I couldn't wait. I had been waiting so long to play at my ability once again, pain-free.

Then it hit me: After going to practice and trying to get back into the swing of things, unfortunately things didn't go as planned. At first I had no knee pain and it felt amazing, and then all the sudden I wasn't pain-free anymore. Come to think of it, my knee would never be the same again. I didn't understand because I was thinking after this second knee surgery it would fix everything, but that was not the case. Since I never had the proper knee surgery from the start, it caused more damage to the knee because the main issue wasn't fixed. When it came to my second knee surgery, they tried to fix what was messed up but my knee was already too damaged from coming back and playing on it when it wasn't fixed properly. Every day this brought me down. I cried so many days and nights. It hurt because I had given everything I had and it seemed as if nobody had my back, and now I must live with this the rest of my life.

I couldn't understand but something inside of me wouldn't give up. I continued to practice, but soon I learned that there was no way possible for me to practice and play games. I had to choose, and of course I'd rather play than to practice. Most people would have been happy to not practice and just play games, but not me. In fact, there were many days in practice where I would ride the stationary bike and cry. Usually two to three times a week I would go to physical therapy to help with the pain, and usually once a week I got dry-needled in my thighs to help release pressure around the knee.

Dry needle is also known as Intramuscular Stimulation (IMS) which is a very thin needle that is used to stimulate trigger points in the body and helps to produce electrical stimulation which aids in releasing the contracted muscles that cause pain. I was also given cortisone shots to help ease the pain and inflammation in my knee.

Eventually it would come to a point where I had to figure out how long I could play each quarter. I couldn't play a full game without having a sub. When I would sub out I would go lie down at the end of the bench and roll out my quads on a roller. Let me just say I had the best sub ever, Malaka Frank. Malaka was a freshman, and I know how it is to be new to a program and come in and get minutes. At every practice and every game, I would talk to her about her roles and how she could become a better player. If you just talk to someone and guide them, there's a lot someone can bring to the table. Not once did I worry when she came in for me, because she knew what was expected and that was to play hard and sacrifice for the team.

After a while of testing out my body, my trainer along with Coach Clark-Heard and I concluded that it would be best for me to play five minutes per quarter so that I was able to bring what I had to the court as well as finish out the games. This was hard for me. The fact that I couldn't practice like everyone else, play in games as much as I wanted to and I was still in the starting lineup bothered me more than anything. It had already bothered me considering that I was transferring from UK - I didn't want anyone to think that I was better than anyone else. Even though Coach would tell me "I don't care what others think, I know what's best for the team" my emotions wouldn't allow me to feel the way she did. I didn't want my teammates mad at me, and I knew people would talk. I didn't want to disappoint anyone, I just wanted to help. Every time I stepped on the court and watched everyone play to their best abilities I felt like a failure, I felt like I couldn't do what they did, I felt like they brought more value to the team because their bodies were able to do what was asked of it, and I couldn't understand why.

I just wanted all of this to go away, but I was already in this dark room and it was like there was no escaping. Who have I become? What is wrong with me?

CHAPTER 9

At first I didn't know I was depressed. I had heard about it before but never really knew much about it. I was "too happy" to ever be depressed, or so I thought.

What made me depressed was that I felt like no one ever listened to me. Maybe if someone would have taken the time to listen I would've never been in that position. My basketball career was slipping away from me way too fast. I became bitter. I literally went to class and practice, then came home to lie in bed all day. The only way that I could get motivated and start my day was by popping an

Adderall to get me through the day. I was prescribed Adderall my freshman year at Kentucky when I was diagnosed with ADD, which is Attention Deficit Disorder. If you don't know what Adderall is, it is a medication that is given to people who have ADD or ADHD (Attention Deficit Hyperactivity Disorder). It is used to treat both children and adults.

I had always heard that people could get addicted to Adderall but I refused to do so. Little did I know, Adderall was starting to become my ole reliable friend. It was the only thing that could keep me distracted from all the heartbreak and pain I was dealing with. It allowed me to just focus on basketball and get better while numbing all the physical and mental pain. Was the physical pain really numb? No, but it allowed me to push myself through the pain. If I'm real with you by this time I didn't even know who I was anymore. I was fighting this demon in my head and I was very depressed. Also I had already lost 25 pounds - I looked sick. I was at the lowest point that I had ever been. I didn't even know how to deal with my feelings anymore because I kept them all balled up. I was afraid to talk to anyone about them. At this point I honestly didn't even feel like my feelings mattered so I kept them to myself. Since I had refused to show any sign of weakness, I continued wearing my mask that had a smile on it.

Every day I would wake up and fake a smile to get me through classes and practice. I don't even know how I made it through the season. All I knew was that I had promised my coach that I would win her a conference championship so I felt like I had to get it done. It's the only thing that got me through the year. In the back of my mind winning that championship for my coach and teammates is what I knew I had to do. What I didn't know was how much more time I had left in me, but I was determined to get it done that season.

To this day, I don't know how I finished out that season, I truly don't. All I know is God's hand had to have been placed on that basketball season to work a miracle. And, just as I had promised coach at the beginning of the season, our team won the C-USA Conference Championship! We did it! I was so glad because I hated promising something and breaking a promise. Maybe that was the grace of God.

Winning the Conference USA title was important for us because we needed that win in order to compete in March Madness, the best time of the year. Our team was selected to play against Ohio State University in the first round of the NCAA. I was happy because I would be getting a chance to play against my old teammate Linnae Harper, who had also transferred from UK the same year I did. Not to mention, in our bracket was Ohio State

University (Linnae Harper), Western Kentucky University (myself), and University of Kentucky (Makayla Epps). We played in Lexington, Kentucky at Memorial Coliseum. I thought this was one of the coolest things. I mean, what are the odds of the Top Five class in the Nation splitting up and playing in the same bracket in the same location? I knew it wouldn't be easy playing because my knee was shot to pieces, not including my left knee which had already started giving me problems due to overcompensating when my right knee was hurting, but I wasn't going to give up that easily. I was going to fight to the very end. The game was very intense. Ohio was ranked 5th in the tournament and we were ranked 12th. I came out thinking that we would give them an upset. But by the second half I was fighting to finish and I was no longer on fire. My playing time in this game had increased, and it was starting to show. I was in serious pain, but I refused to rest until the buzzer sounded off.

Sadly, we lost in the first round of the NCAA tournament with the final score Western Kentucky 63 Ohio State 70.

I just wanted to cry. After the game I felt horrible - a quitter, worthless, sad, let down, lost and confused. I already knew what was coming next, but nobody else did. Will they understand? Will they still accept me? Will I be considered a quitter if do what I think is best for me?

CHAPTER 10

And just like that, the season was over.

What would happen next no one would
understand. I had come to the conclusion that it
was time for me to stop playing basketball because
I knew that I couldn't take it anymore. I couldn't
bear taking the knee pain while pretending to be
happy, and I had to make a choice. After playing
basketball for the past 18 years of my life, I had to
tell family, friends, and my coach that I would not
be able to play my last eligibility year. This was a
hard decision to make, but I had to because I never
fully recovered from my first surgery and my body
was starting to shut down.

Do you know how hard it is to walk away from something that has been a part of your life for the past 18 years? Gosh, like when you really love something and it's taken away from you, it becomes a hard pill to swallow. Not to mention, I had so many people mad at me for my decision. They didn't know what I was going through, but never took the time to, but that could also be because I never gave them the time to understand. I was suffering in silence, whatever was thrown at me I just took it. I never let anyone see my pain. I never let anyone know what I was battling mentally, they only saw what I was battling physically. I didn't want to be labeled as weak.

The back lash I got for not playing my last year had me crying for a while. People very close to me said that I was pathetic for not taking my last year of basketball. "People are trying to do what you do every day and here you are trying to quit. You're selfish!" I couldn't understand why no one understood. I'm in excruciating pain and I don't know how much more I can take. Not only am I in pain physically, but I'm in pain mentally. I'm about to give up the game of basketball, something that I truly love and you're mad at me? Everything I've gone through for this sport, do you think it's easy to give up? No! Look and see what's *really* going on because you never really know what someone is going through.

I felt like I had failed and that I didn't know anything that I was supposed to do. I look back on my resume and see all the championships that I've had and could see that I was a winner. I mean hell, I promised Coach Clark-Heard a championship the day I stepped in her office, but in the back of my mind the whole time I was scared I had promised her something too soon, because I knew my knee was in bad condition. I didn't know how bad it was until after the season had begun and I was no longer practicing but only playing games. I can barely walk some days.

Now it was time to tell my coach that I decided not to play my last year at Western. My mindset going into the office was "It's okay, we got a championship. It's okay to take time for you, Kyvin..."

I sat down at her desk and told her I didn't think I was going to play my last year. I explained to her how much pain I was in and that I just couldn't do it any longer. We talked a little more and said our goodbyes. I still couldn't believe that I was walking away from basketball. I couldn't believe it had come to this point - that I was being forced to walk away from playing. Why does it have to be like this and go through this much pain?

My depression was getting worse by the day.

CHAPTER 11

Once I had graduated from Western Kentucky University in 2017 I decided to move back home to Campbellsville, Kentucky. I didn't even attend my own graduation - I just wanted my diploma to be sent through the mail. I moved in with my cousin Shakila who has literally been by my side since I arrived in this world. While at home I worked at a day care. I've known the owners of the day care since I was a kid. When I was in middle school they owned a store that I used to go to almost every morning before school, and that store was later converted into a day care. I couldn't pass up the opportunity to teach and play with kids all day.

I worked there for a couple months until one day I got a call from Coach Mark Campbell. He had called me a couple months prior and asked me to come play for him at Union University, located in Jackson, Tennessee (a Division II school about four hours away from Campbellsville). Sara Hammond, his assistant coach, told him about me and he decided to reach out. Sara was my former teammate from Kentucky Premier AAU team. After AAU, she attended the University of Louisville where she was on an athletic basketball scholarship and later went on to play professionally overseas. He tried talking me into playing my last eligibility year and at first I told him no.

But here was Coach Campbell and Sara Hammond calling again asking the same question but this time they said something that caught my attention. They began to tell me they thought if I came there I would be going there for something more than just basketball. I'm sitting here thinking, what do you mean something bigger than basketball? How can something be bigger than just basketball? Is this one of those tricks again? I ain't got time! I'm sorry but that just how I was thinking. But after five months of telling them "no" I eventually gave in and told Coach Campbell, "I'll come on a visit."

Let's just say I'm glad I went on the visit. I hadn't been in that type of environment in my life. Everything was so peaceful, but honestly, I was scared to attend there. It was a Christian school and I didn't have much "Holy" inside me at the time. I mean, I'm a nice person and I like to help people but I didn't know much about the "Christian" thing. I grew up in a Baptist church that I eventually stopped going to once I started getting older and was always on-the-go for basketball. Plus, I never understood the Bible when I tried to read it, but I just knew there was a God that I believed in. I just didn't know much about Him. I knew I wasn't perfect and I wasn't sure if my teammates would accept me. I don't know, I just had some crazy thoughts I guess because it was a Christian school and I was just a little uncomfortable at first.

In other words, I went back to school... again. My third school.

My mindset had been messed up about basketball for a while. Thank goodness for Sara. She had been watching and decided to take a chance on me. Whenever I asked her what made her ask me to come to Union, she responded, "First I just wanted to make sure I was keeping up with you and how you were doing. Once I saw you decided not to play anymore, Coach Campbell said he needed someone with experience & leadership. You instantly came to my mind and I knew you loved the game of basketball and I wanted you to be able to finish your basketball career on a high note, go out without any regret or doubt.

Secondly, I knew how much Coach Campbell and Union had changed my mindset and heart of my identity not being in basketball but in Christ. From your experiences at UK I knew Union was a place that could transform your heart and give you a new perspective on life and the love God has for us no matter what we endure in this life.

So, to sum it all up I guess I wanted you to have an enjoyable college playing experience and to get to be a part of a team and University that is so different in how we love one another."

CHAPTER 12

At the time, I didn't know how God worked.

He had been watching over me the whole time and

not only was He watching over me, He was listening

too. Every question that I had been asking up until I

got to Union, He answered. I would always ask, why

isn't anyone listening? Why did I have to go through

what I went through? Why does basketball feel like

it's slipping away? Why have I been treated the way

that I've been treated after giving everything that I

had? It was confusing and frustrating. Out of all the

things that I said during my college playing career,

the one thing I would always remember saying

constantly was that nobody else could be going

through what I'm going through. What I didn't know was that God was going to show me everything that I wanted answers to plus more during my time at Union. When Coach Campbell said he thought I was coming for more reasons other than just basketball, I now know what he meant. He honestly changed my life. Not only was he a coach that had won national championships, but he knew how to invest in his players.

Coach Campbell told me "I knew that what you were looking for was to be loved and cared for within the sport that you have loved all your life. Through our conversations, through your social media posts. I knew that your heart was soft, you cared for others and therefore you wanted to be treated that same way. Ultimately, I knew that Union, we could provide exactly what had been missing in your basketball experience. We are not perfect but our motive is to love."

By coming to Union I was able to realize that what I had been asking for wasn't too much. It made me love the game again. I could see that everything that I had been through so far had made me stronger and that there was a good meaning behind it all. At the end of the day Coach Campbell knew how to get the best out of his players and never once made his job about him, never once became selfish and forgot the true meaning of coaching. He cared about his players more than just basketball.

After four long hours of driving I finally arrived on campus. My new teammates and coach helped me unpack my car and carry my stuff inside my new room. If you know me you know that I'm shy so sometimes it takes me a while to warm up to people. I was in a whole new state with people I've only known for a month or so, and I had no clue as to why I was there. I was still at a point where I didn't even want to watch basketball on television, let alone play anymore. I hadn't forgotten how I felt my last game and I didn't want to feel that pain ever again. I'm clearly very crippled, why in the world am I still trying to play basketball? I've got to be crazy. Why does Coach Campbell want to take a chance on a cripple? I'm not sure if I will even last a semester and if I do, this is going to be crucial.

In the back of my mind I'm still thinking about how Coach Campbell told me I was here for more than just basketball, that's pretty much the only thing that kept me motivated. All I knew was I was searching for happiness and answers, and in that fall semester I would find everything my soul had been seeking for. Prayer works.

CHAPTER 13

Campus was empty. Everyone had already gone home for the holidays. Fall sports were the only ones still left on campus. We had practice later that day but I couldn't practice yet because I still had to get my medical records from my previous schools. Once those came in I had to get my check-ups and see the bone and joint specialist before I could even touch the court.

After sitting in the waiting room to see the doctor, they finally called me back. The doctor and I chatted about my knee history and then he began to do MRI's, X-rays and some other test on my knees. Once he had the results, he gave me a shaky look. Instantly I started doubting myself, like what was I doing here? What was I thinking? This was dumb of me to even come here and attempt to play basketball.

Then he smiled, saying, "You're really about to play basketball on this knee? I'm not even sure how you're still playing!" I was thinking the same thing he was, but hearing it from the doctor made me worry even more. How bad is my knee right now? When I left from Western Kentucky they had already told me I had 50-year old knee from all the damage, what is it now, 80 years old?

It was December, which meant there were about four months left of basketball, and he was wondering if I would make it through. We wrapped

up the appointment, and by the time I left there,

we both knew we would be seeing each other

several times throughout the season. I didn't care

though. For the first time in a while I felt like I could

really trust a doctor. With my many questions, he

was a very honest and genuine person. I didn't

really have much fear. I was quickly gaining my trust

with him. All of the answers that I had been

wanting to know about my ability, he was able to

answer. He helped me understand why I had gone

through what I had been through. He even felt the

pain I was dealing with knowing that my first

surgery hadn't been done correctly, but I knew I

was in good hands so the worries started to leave fast.

After watching a couple of practices, I was finally able to touch the floor. For the first time in my life, on the court, I felt fear. I no longer had the confidence that I used to have. I was scared my teammates would look at me and wonder how I ever even touched the floor at the D1 level. This was just my anxiety kicking in, it's not really what they thought but that's how I felt when I stepped on the court to play. I also didn't want anyone thinking I was there to take their place because in reality I was still trying to figure out what I was doing there.

Instead, everyone was very welcoming and understanding of my situation. As it turned out, everyone already knew my background because Coach had talked to them about me. No one judged me, no one ever gave up on me. They all accepted me for who I was and never looked at me any differently.

It didn't take long for me to adjust to the system. I quickly became comfortable around everyone. Practices had been going well and it was almost time for me to finally play a game. A couple of days right before it was time for me to make my first appearance in my debut game I got hurt. During practice we were scrimmaging, and I went to contest a shot and when I came down, I came down all wrong. I laid there for a second and then said, "I'm good" but when I tried to get up it was like something pulled me back down. I had a sharp pain shooting through my lower back and every time I would try to get up it prevented me. My teammates, trainer and coach all ran over to help me up. I sat down and finished watching practice while I iced my back. I was so mad. But as usual I continued to smile. The next day I went to get my back checked out and they put me on meds and recommended I sit out for a week. I'm thinking, a week? I'll be back in like two days, what are you talking about? Unfortunately, I had to wait a week because by the second day the pain stayed the same.

Coach and I talked about what happened and we shared a couple of laughs. I told him I would be fine and I'll come back as soon as possible, but then he smiled and said "Stop worrying. Rest. It's okay." What? You're not rushing me back? This was one of the weirdest moments for me, I wasn't expecting this answer. I'm used to being pushed - not told rest. On the inside I was looking at him a little crazy but smiling on the outside. I told him okay and did what he said, even though I really wasn't trying to hear the word rest. That stuck with me for a while. For the first time in my life I was looking at life a little differently. In four years, I don't think I've ever really rested. Yes, I had my off days, lazy days, etc. but I still never rested. My mind never let me rest. I was trained to work for what you wanted and if I was resting physically then my mind was running 1000 mph worrying about if I'm pushing myself to be the best I can be, if I'm doing enough, and will I ever be enough.

I always felt guilty if I rested. Over the course of four years that's how my brained had trained itself. Coach Campbell made me feel like it was okay to rest and from that moment on not only did I choose to rest because of my injury, but I realized that it was time to also start working on my mental well-being so that I could learn how to bring that to rest as well.

Another thing I brought to rest was my Adderrall habit - actually I'd stopped taking it when the season had ended at Western Kentucky. This was definitely a positive step in the right direction because I no longer felt that it was the only way to get through the day. I was able to control my mind and live more freely. When I stopped taking Adderrall I also noticed I had issues with anxiety. During the time that I was on the medication, I never really paid that much attention to my anxiety because Adderrall kept me distracted from it. But since I was more aware of my anxiety, I could manage it properly. It was a great feeling to see that I was finally conquering my demons that had taken over my life in the last year and getting back to my regular self.

CHAPTER 14

After sitting out for a week due to my back injury, it was time to finally play my first game. For the first time in a long time, I got that butterfly feeling that you get when you play your first game back. Although it felt normal playing, it wasn't long before all my pain started coming back and here I was fighting a mental battle again. Thankfully, I had a good support group surrounding me that helped guide me into a more stable mindset about my situation.

Throughout the season, I quickly had to understand that I had to bring something else to this team. I learned that it was not only my athletic ability that I needed to bring, but my leadership skills. During my time at Union I was teaching sacrifice through my actions. Everyone knew that I shouldn't have been on the court that year, but there was more to the story that people from the outside looking in didn't understand. Every game was a battle, but I knew this wasn't just about me. It was also about the people who surrounded me and the Man upstairs. I needed to learn who I was, and that everything that had happened to me didn't define me. I needed to learn that I do not belong to this world but to a different kingdom and so I couldn't identify myself into the things of this world including basketball (thanks to my teammates and coaches who helped me understand this along our journey). While I was learning about the meaning of life my teammates

were learning something from me as well. I didn't

see it this way until about tournament time, but

apparently, my actions were speaking louder than

my words. Every game I was demonstrating

sacrifice.

For years, I had never seen it this way until they

opened my eyes. Despite everything that I had been

through, I was able to look back on all the sacrifices

that I had made, not just for me but for the ones

around me. Every time my teammates and I went

to battle I sacrificed my body each time. I would

take the hardest hits for my teammates. Behind

closed doors I was the one who would sit down and

discuss with the coach about opinions that my teammates and I would have. Anything to help my teammates achieve their goals I would try and help. I may not have come out and told them what I was doing because I've always been the type to keep things to myself, but whether they saw it through my actions or not it was never really for me. It had always been about the ones that surrounded me. Now as I look back that might explain my many championships.

During one of our games I dove for a ball and went head-first into the bleachers. Needless to say, I suffered a concussion. I walked over to the gym to go through my concussion protocol. I was checking to see if I could watch practice that day but was quickly turned down after failing my concussion test again. As I was walking down the hallway to go back to my room, I stopped by our Graduate Assistant's office with whom I had become very close to. As usual she said my name with a smile. I sat down and we talked as we usually did. She asked if I was coming to practice, and with a grumpy look on my face I said no. She then asked me if I was going to Pensacola Florida with the team for our game against University of West Florida. I told her I wasn't sure, it depended on if the doctor would clear me due to my concussion.

We talked some more and then she proceeded to tell me that she was planning on getting baptized in the ocean while in Pensacola. I got super excited and told her I would join her. She looked and me and said "Really?" I said "Yes!" I asked her who was going to baptize her and she said Coach Campbell. We hurried off to Coach Campbell's office to ask if I could join and get baptized also. Coach Campbell had the biggest smile on his face and was very excited that I decided to dedicate my life to Christ. There was only one problem – would I be able to go on the team trip? At the moment I still wasn't cleared to travel due to my concussion. I started to worry but I quickly changed my mindset and went to my trainer to inform her of our plans and was wondering if she thought the doctor would let me travel. But of course, I had to wait until my next checkup so I just started to pray hoping that I would get to travel with the team so I could get baptized and support my teammates at the game. It was crazy to me because I would always get these visions of getting baptized in the ocean, and here was my chance for my vision to become true.

A couple of days passed and the day before it was time to hit the road with the team I was cleared to travel. We had about a 7-hour drive to Pensacola Florida. Once we arrived we went to a seafood place on the beach to eat. After everyone had finished eating, the team, coaches and other Union supporters walked down to the ocean and prepared for my and Trina's baptism. Before we were baptized some of my teammates and Union supporters said some kind words and read some of their favorite scriptures from the Bible. I was nervous but I was ready for a new outlook on my life, and I was ready to dedicate my life to something way more than basketball. It was the greatest moment of my life. It was great being baptized by a caring and loving coach who understood that there were more important things in life besides just the game of basketball, which explains why he's been so successful in his career.

After the baptism, we all gathered back on to the bus and headed over to the University of West Florida's gym to prepare for basketball practice. While the team practiced, I rode the bike. I had to sit out because of my concussion. But as I sat there and road the bike, I sat there in peace; something I hadn't felt in a long time. I couldn't believe what had just happened, but I was thankful that God answered my prayers and placed me in a loving, caring, supportive environment where I knew I would leave and become successful because of the effort and time that my coaches and teammates put in me. If it weren't for Union University I honestly don't know where I would be today.

CHAPTER 15

We went on to win the Gulf South Conference Regular Season and Conference Tournament as well as the South Region Championship. We held the Quarterfinals, Region Quarter Finals, and the Region Finals on our home court. It felt even better winning all three of the games at home. We couldn't rest though - we still had one more tournament to conquer.

After all the hard work and sacrifices we had made it to the NCAA Division II Women's Basketball National Elite Tournament in Sioux Falls, South Dakota. We played Carson-Newman University which we defeated 73-30 to help us advance to the

Elite Eight. Next up we would face University of Central Missouri who we would lose to in the Final Four (57-70). It hurt at first and of course we cried. I knew this was going to be my last game, and I knew I had given everything that I had and so did my teammates. We ended up finishing #4 in the NCAA Division II Women's Basketball Coaches Association poll.

But what some people didn't realize was Coach had never even expected to get that far in the season based off the previous season and many of the players' injuries. Even though we had lost he showed us the bigger picture. He sat down with us in the locker room and expressed that it was a very successful season not because of our winning record but because of the sacrifices and growth everyone had made, and everything we had been through to get to where we were. We had three seniors with bad knees and many different knee surgeries, one senior who had hip surgery and at first didn't want to come back and play basketball due to her chronic pain; another senior sitting out from tearing her ACL earlier in the season and the list goes on but you get the point. At the end of the day we had beaten the odds and so we knew we couldn't hang our heads. I had overcome a lot mentally as well thanks to that season. I was able to find myself again due to Coach always reminding us "Basketball is what you do, it's not who you are."

For first time in years I could understand the true meaning of basketball, and it wasn't about winning games. It was about helping the people along the way, building character and sacrificing. I had always demonstrated these things in my game, but for the first time in my life I felt like it was appreciated. Sometimes in life people take things for granted and forget the true meaning of life. It's not just about winning games but bettering the people around you so that they can win on the court and at life.

You will never be able to win in life if you start putting your identity into the things of this world. That's why it's important to be careful who you encounter, because if you are being led by someone who has forgotten the true meaning of life - being tied up into impressing people and just making themselves look good and trying to fit into a system - you may fall into the same trap. Then when things begin to fall apart you will begin to lose yourself; all because you decided to let a sport, person, a loved one, a school, or an opinion define you. Whatever happens to you happens to you for a reason. What happened to you is not who you are, it just happened and it more than likely happened for a reason. So, don't say why me? Say try me! Try to see what you're going through and what it's trying to teach you.

If you have ever been through or are going through something like what I've been through just know that you have a voice, and you are allowed to speak on it. Don't feel as if you must hold everything in because you don't want to hurt anybody's feelings. It's okay to express how you feel, it's not healthy holding things back. You will become freer after you let how you feel off your chest. Not everyone is going to agree with you and that is fine. But you must stand up for what you think is right. If you know you're not in a good environment, know that it is okay to walk away. Don't get so attached to the seasonal things. Those things come and go. Some things come in for a season, some come for a reason. Make sure you know the difference.

Know that because you choose to walk away from different people, things, teams, loved ones for the better doesn't make you weak, and it won't interfere with your future, because at the end of the day what is for you will always be for you. Your route might look different than the next person, but we were all created differently for a reason. Trust God's plans over your emotions.

CHAPTER 16

Before I left Union University, I was

scheduled to have my third knee surgery on May 1,

2018. That's right - my third one. The only

difference between this one and the other two is

that my first two were on my right knee and this

surgery was for my left knee. That evening was our

basketball banquet. It was kind of bittersweet in

the fact that I would be leaving some wonderful

people that I had met during my five months at

Union. I couldn't believe that the same school that

I kept turning down to Coach Campbell ended up

being the very school that changed me forever.

When I look back on it, I'm glad I took that chance,

and I'm very grateful for the relationships and bonds that were built along the way.

When the banquet ended and I said my goodbyes to my coach and teammates, I headed back to Kentucky the same night. It would take about nine months to a year to recover and get full mobility back in my knee.

At this point, I pretty much knew that once I left Union, and especially after having had my third knee surgery, that it would be my last time playing basketball. Even though I thought it was over after I left from Western Kentucky, I still had a year of eligibility left that I was able to finish. But this time, I knew this was it. Sometimes I thought about trying to go overseas and play pro, but I no longer felt the need to do so. I felt like it would be better using my talents toward younger kids and being a role model. I wanted to help them know how to get to the next level.

Through my basketball journey, it has shaped me into the person that I am today. Many people think basketball may just be a sport that is about being physical and winning, but I think it is way more than that. With sports, you are able to learn real world life skills that you need to apply in your life. You learn to work hard and believe in yourself, you learn how to be selfless and work in a group, how to overcome adversity as well as other valuable lessons. Because of my journey through basketball I know how to connect with others and get the best out of them. What had happened to me through my journey was preparing me for my coaching days.

I like coaching because it allows you to bring the best out of people. It's a great way to build relationships. My experience has taught me to listen to my players' opinions, because everyone's opinion matters. I made a promise to myself to always be the coach that players aren't afraid to build a relationship with and always coach with a purpose. My experience allowed me to learn that things aren't always going to go your way so be patient and don't get mad at outcomes. Instead, look at the bigger picture and take time to reflect.

Don't let your emotions take over, remember an

emotion is an emotion don't let it keep you from

doing the right thing. I will teach my players how to

have a great work ethic when it comes to their skill

and character. I will make sure that I instill

character to my players and make sure they learn

how to hold themselves accountable, as well as the

ones that surround them, because at the end of the

day it is a team thing so we all must buy into the

system.

I want my players to be the best that they can be on

and off the court. I want them to do their best

every day and always push through when adversity

hits, in other words never give up. Basketball is more than just a game. Basketball helps build character, the type of character that you are going to need to make it through life. When I coach, I'm not just coaching for myself. I'm coaching for the ones around me and their future.

CHAPTER 17

To get a glimpse into what the sports in college is like, along with the many sacrifices we make, I interviewed some former college basketball players with whom I've had the great pleasure of knowing through the game of basketball. They give their depiction of the student-athlete experience - the ups, the downs, the highs, and the lows. Through it all, each were able to persevere and become successful; not only in college, but also in life.

"People have always asked me, 'Hey Epps, what's it like being a college athlete?' And at first I just chuckle a little because that is a hard and difficult question to answer and every athlete may have a different answer for you. But I am here to tell you that being a college athlete is both a blessing and a curse in a sense.

It's a blessing because you earned a scholarship to attend college and continue to pursue your dreams (a definite plus and major positive for any athlete). College scholarships aren't just passed out to any and everybody, you must earn that. So when it's earned, you sign and have your signing party and all of that. It is a tremendous feeling and pivotal moment in a college athlete's life.

Then things get real. Late nights, early mornings. 5 AM workouts, followed by class, tutors, study hall, practices, weights, training tables, traveling, treatment, workouts, etc. Being a college student athlete can become overwhelming. It's a lot to take in and process as a 17-18yr old kid. You have to sacrifice missing holidays with families. Sacrifice weekends with your friends doing other things you like. You sacrifice your time, your mental well-being, your body, and a lot more.

I struggled coming into college. The game was faster, players were better than me, bigger, smarter, etc. It was very frustrating, coming out of high school as a top-rated prospect and all this clout and hype. But none of that mattered when I got to UK. They didn't care who I was, where I was from, what I did in high school or who my dad was. Everything I achieved at UK, I earned. It had to be earned. I worked for it. I used to bust my tail freshman year and only played in like 10 games out of 30. That's rough when you're used to playing, producing, and being on the court. So my freshman year I battled many demons inside and out.

My college experience was a rollercoaster. Up and downs. Freshman year I was low. Sophomore year I was on an upscale, junior year I was high, and then senior year, after a lot of turmoil, I wasn't as high as my junior year, but not as low as my freshman year, but there was a decline in myself and I felt it.... But I wouldn't want to re-do or have it any other way!!!

The things I have went through- mentally, physically, and emotionally have shaped me to be the young woman I am currently! I thank the University of Kentucky for taking a shot on a young kid with nothing but a ball and a dream from Lebanon, KY. I also thank UK for all of the valuable life lessons and blessings I've learned and acquired along the way.

To my future college athletes: MAKE THE CHOICE BEST FOR YOU! I wish you nothing but the absolute best on your future endeavors and if you ever need somebody to talk to, I'm all over social media, so reach out, I'd love to help as much as I can in any way."

Makayla Epps
————————

"My collegiate career was definitely a story. I've learned so much on and off the court and it has definitely shaped me into the person I am today. Throughout college I struggled with confidence, courage, and battling with my mental thoughts but I was able to fight through and overcome everything - despite the good, the bad and the ugly. I've built some amazing relationship with people that I will forever cherish and love! My teammates and others were like my family away from home and we stuck together like a family through thick and thin, and I think that helped me with getting through college better.

Sometimes you have to fight your battles alone as sometimes you have to go to war with the people by yourself that you love the most. I even questioned if I wanted to play basketball during college but I had to remember all the people that were rooting for me and touting for my success. So through it all, everything happened for a reason and I'm happy everything worked out the way it did."

Linnae Harper

— — — — — —

"To be a student-athlete is unlike anything else that I've experienced in my life. I always dreamed of playing at the next level, but I have to admit that I wasn't aware of the sacrifice and dedication that it required of me. When my dreams became a reality, I soon after realized that I was the property of a university. I no longer had a life of my own. Early morning training sessions while the rest of the student body was still asleep, early classes to make way for mid-day practices, and a curfew were just a snippet of what my daily life consisted of. Not to mention, travel and missing classes due to games. At times the make-up work was brutal.

I struggled with being so far away from home as a freshman. The hometown crowd that once cheered me on was miles away and I was eager for their support. My first year was difficult to say the least. The team was made up of veteran players, however I outplayed and out-hustled them all, causing friction amongst my teammates. The head coach did not defuse the situation and allowed things to become so uncomfortable for me that I transferred at the end of the season.

What I thought was a new beginning my sophomore year, ended up being a total disaster due to no fault of my own. The team was suspended shortly after I arrived on campus and I was forced to shop myself around, once again, to another school. I refused to give up on my dream, no matter what obstacles were thrown at me. I knew that I would end up exactly where God intended.

My junior year brought me back home to my hometown and to the school that owns my heart. Unlike the other two universities, this one didn't offer me a full scholarship. I was forced to be a walk-on (which is a nice name for a practice player). My confidence took a hit, but my love for the game wouldn't allow me to give up on myself. During this time, I was also introduced to student loans. The financial obligations were overwhelming, but I understood that my role as a practice player could eventually earn me a scholarship. I also understood that playing for the university would bring them exposure, which would lead to revenue. I used them as a way to get an education, just as they used me to make a profit. It was at this time that I realized the business aspects of college sports.

My senior year brought financial blessings. My tuition was paid in full, along with housing, meal plan and books. I was traveling again; seeing the world. I regained my confidence with the help of my teammates and coaching staff. I was a part of a team; one in which I will always be proud to call my family.

The game of basketball has been my life line. My faith teaches me that learning to love is the single most important lesson in life and my love for this game has led me to lifelong friendships. I can only hope that this sport will be a blessing for others as it has been for me."

Jamil Shanklin

————————

"Fourteen points, 4 assists in 30 minutes of action at #24 Texas A&M on January 4, 2018. It was after this game I almost quit playing mid-season and had a full-out mental breakdown. This was the last I could take. The entire day before the game I had cried so much my eyes were swollen. I had barely managed to eat our pre-game meal, but I hadn't been able to eat much for awhile. When I got home the next day, my dad took me out for a nice dinner to talk some "sense" into me. I remember forcing myself to dress semi-nice and apply some makeup - things that had become less and less frequent for me. I remember being really quiet for most of that meal and trying to find joy in this moment since at least I didn't have to be at the gym. I can still feel what I was like in that very moment. Numb. Confused. Alone. Ready to run and not stop. I could not live life this way anymore. I only gave you my stats of that game to show things are never as they seem. Thank God for last straws. Somewhere in the midst of our lowest points we have no choice but to face whatever we've been avoiding. There I was, staring straight at it. There was no hiding anymore.

I'm going to get brutally honest. You are going to know a part of me I have let few know in years. "It's really none of your business. You wouldn't understand." That's what selfish me says. When I say "What if they judge?" God says, "I don't. You could save someone's life. You are eternally loved, you are eternally free to be all I have made you to be. Imperfections and all." So here I am. An open book. *For most of my college athletic career I have quietly battled a loud depression.* It single-handedly robbed me of experiencing joy - a joy that God wants me to have daily. I'm not sure if this is something I would have struggled with had I not chosen to play a sport in college, all I can share is a story of someone who's done both at the same time: Battled depression and played basketball at a major Division I school. I know God did not allow me to go through this to hide it forever.

As I learned of some of the same struggles my fellow teammates and friends at other places were going through, I wanted to be like 'I wish we could have talked about this together, sooner.'

Division I basketball, especially at a Power 5 school, has a huge pressure to perform. It's a business at that point. It has a not-so-funny way of making you believe your whole value is in performance. That side of it has its perks too. Having people know you for athletic success is a great feeling. It's a blessing to get free school and benefits. But then you go home and reality sets in that your whole life revolves around tangible things. I have learned that if my life is centered around anything than my relationship with Christ and God's purpose for me, things go south. When I was a little girl that's all I wanted was to play at the highest level and I am so glad I can say I did. But it's tough, man.

I feel like as humans and especially in athletics we really lose perspective of the bigger picture and what really matters. Athletes are put on a pedestal. As a Christian my main goal is to love everyone and share Christ with others. Not run a million miles in a certain time or score a certain amount of points. Or get a certain grade on a test. As long as I'm living out my purpose and loving others as God called me I should be pleased.

Your identity outside of basketball matters. That's a piece of advice a lot of times is not given to younger athletes. Or older ones. Or me. I think who you are outside of your sport or any sport is just as important of a question as what you bring to the table in your athletic field. I can't speak for everyone else, but I know for me, and surely others, it is a huge reason on top of other medical reasons that I struggled severely. The athletic world tells you that you need to be the best. But they also tell you you're never going to achieve the best. Work harder. Not good enough. But you never will achieve that. Someone else is always better. But the truth of the matter...you are also the best.

I am so thankful I am loved unconditionally by a God who never left me behind. I'm grateful for healing and freedom. I don't know what life looks like for me now, and I've given up trying to decide it for myself. My life is yours, God. I'm trusting You will bring me better. Through the hurt I trust You. I'm thankful for people who showed me love whenever I didn't think I could be loved. Please do not be afraid to speak up. Please do not be afraid to check on your friends. Do not be afraid to seek help. There's freedom for me, and there's freedom for you. I'm tired of hiding. So there it is."

Makenzie Cann

——————

"Transforming from high school basketball to college basketball was a crazy adjustment. In high school I always stayed in somebody's gym getting up shots and practicing on moves for the games. I knew in order to get to the next level, you have to work hard and it takes dedication. I earned my way to college and it was a crazy 5 years. I went to Middle Tennessee State University for 2 years and transferred after my second year, due to personal reasons. During this transfer process it was pretty tough and wasn't as easy I thought. I went through crazy obstacles as far as feeling down on myself, bad relationships and slight depression, but I always trusted God that He was going to help me overcome these obstacles. Next thing you know I was getting a call back from Florida Gulf Coast University offering me a full scholarship, which was probably one of the best decisions I made. FGCU was a great experience and I learned a lot and overcame a lot while I was there. Now, since graduating, I took a year to get to know myself and hang out with friends and family. I am enjoying the adult work life and working my way into getting back into the basketball scene as far as coaching and helping out AAU teams."

China Dow

—————

She stood on the bridge
In silence and fear
For the demons of darkness
Had driven her here

By Olivia B

Source: https://www.familyfriendpoems.com/poems/sad/depression/

"Depression is who and what we allow it to be. I have struggled with depression and suicidal thoughts since the age of seven. My precious parents unintentionally put tons of pressure on me to perform well in the classroom and on the court, understandably so, being one of the only black kids in a southwest Ohio suburb. I also had to talk a certain way, walk a certain way, dress a certain way, and act a certain way. I couldn't be who I knew I wanted to be.

By 7th or 8th grade, my name had been in every girls' basketball blog in Ohio. Some people were kind, most were absolute monsters. 'She'll never be able to play in college with that attitude' turned into full rides from UCONN and UK, as well as offers from nearly EVERY school in America. 'She definitely won't start at the high school level.' Let's just say that was the furthest thing from reality. But instead of using that as motivation to do better, 'teenage' me became very sad and stopped working on my game as much. I was the type of kid that needed everyone to like and support them and when they didn't, it was 'It must be my fault. I'm not good enough.' The 'I'm not good enough' became my motto for the next 13 years.

I had begun to realize that what I thought were typical adolescent issues (because that's what my parents and both college coaches insisted had to be the problem) was in fact depression when I was 25 years old. My former girlfriend, also a behavioral specialist, was the one to pinpoint nearly each issue: depression, bipolar, depersonalization, borderline personality disorder, and the list continues. All of this stemmed from depression. Having black parents and grandparents, saying the word "depression" is almost like cursing at them. So, I learned to suppress all my feelings. I learned to detach myself from people and my interests because 'No one cares anyway.'

Although it is still a struggle, I learned to challenge my depression by finding interest in things I used to love like walking outdoors and reading. I am also extremely picky with who and what I allow into my system (my mind, body and spirit), but most importantly, I ensure I am being who and what I need to my system. I now take responsibility for my actions, reactions, and feelings, as well as count on my close circle to support and hold me accountable. I recently started therapy to gain even more clarity on who I am and who I am constantly becoming. I encourage anyone and everyone to try therapy! I have been suicidal-thought free for one month now and I pray it continues! When you think you've run out of reasons to stay, I promise you, you can and will always find one more. Never give up. Just stay."

Samarie Walker

I know that what I've been through many

athletes have or are experiencing something

similar, as what these athletes' stories have just

described. This is not something that just happened

to me. I'm here to say SPEAK UP! Someone is out

here in need of your story. It doesn't matter what

platform you have, you and your story matters!

#MoreThanJustaGame

PHILIPPIANS 4:6-7 NEW LIVING TRANSLATION (NLT)

6 Don't worry about anything; instead, pray about everything. Tell God what you need, and thank Him for all He has done. 7 Then you will experience God's peace, which exceeds anything we can understand. His peace will guard your hearts and minds as you live in Christ Jesus.

ISAIAH 54:17 7 NEW LIVING TRANSLATION (NLT)

But in that coming day no weapon turned against you will succeed. You will silence every voice raised up to accuse you. These benefits are enjoyed by the servants of the LORD; their vindication will come from me. I, the LORD, have spoken!

KYWEAR

Keeping You Wise Eager And Ready

Spreading positivity, inspiration and guidance throughout the world. KYWEAR helps empower people to be positive through their journey in life as well as influence the culture in a inspirational, loving way.

KYWEAR wants to be a voice of positive thoughts that lead others to do the same. KYWEAR is motivated by Keeping You Wise Eager And Ready.

Instagram: @kywear_

CONTACT ME:

Instagram: @Kyvinn

Twitter: @Kyvinn

Facebook: Kgoodinrogers

Website: www.kyvingoodin-rogers.com

Copyright 2019

Made in the USA
Lexington, KY
09 June 2019